ART OF THE HEART
AND OTHER ANATOMICAL STRUCTURES

A HUMAN ANATOMY COLORING BOOK FOR ALL AGES

by AMY GRACE SLOAN

EDITED BY SIGITA CAHOON, MD & AMY MARCINKOWSKI, MD

> <u>LEARN WHILE YOU PLAY & PLAY WHILE YOU LEARN!</u>
>
> Allow your left and right hemispheres to dance in harmony as you take a break, invite your creativity to the table, and allow yourself a deeper connection with the subject matter. Younger colorists can learn about anatomical structures while they play, anatomy students can take a more meaningful study break and interact with their knowledge in a new way, and more mature colorists can refresh their memories and perhaps learn something new as they experience the joy and relaxation that a good coloring session can bring.

PRINTED BY CREATESPACE, AN AMAZON.COM COMPANY

ISBN-13: 978-1505819731
ISBN-10: 1505819733

Contents

1.   CELL

2.   SKULL

3.   BRAIN

4.   NEURON

5.   EYE

6.   INNER EAR

7.   TOOTH

8.   SKIN

9.   HEART

10.   LUNGS

11.   DIGESTIVE SYSTEM

12.   KIDNEY

13.   BONES OF THE HAND

14.   BONES OF THE FOOT

Please enjoy the extra page in between each image for notes, sketching, testing colors, and protection against color bleed if coloring with markers.

CELL

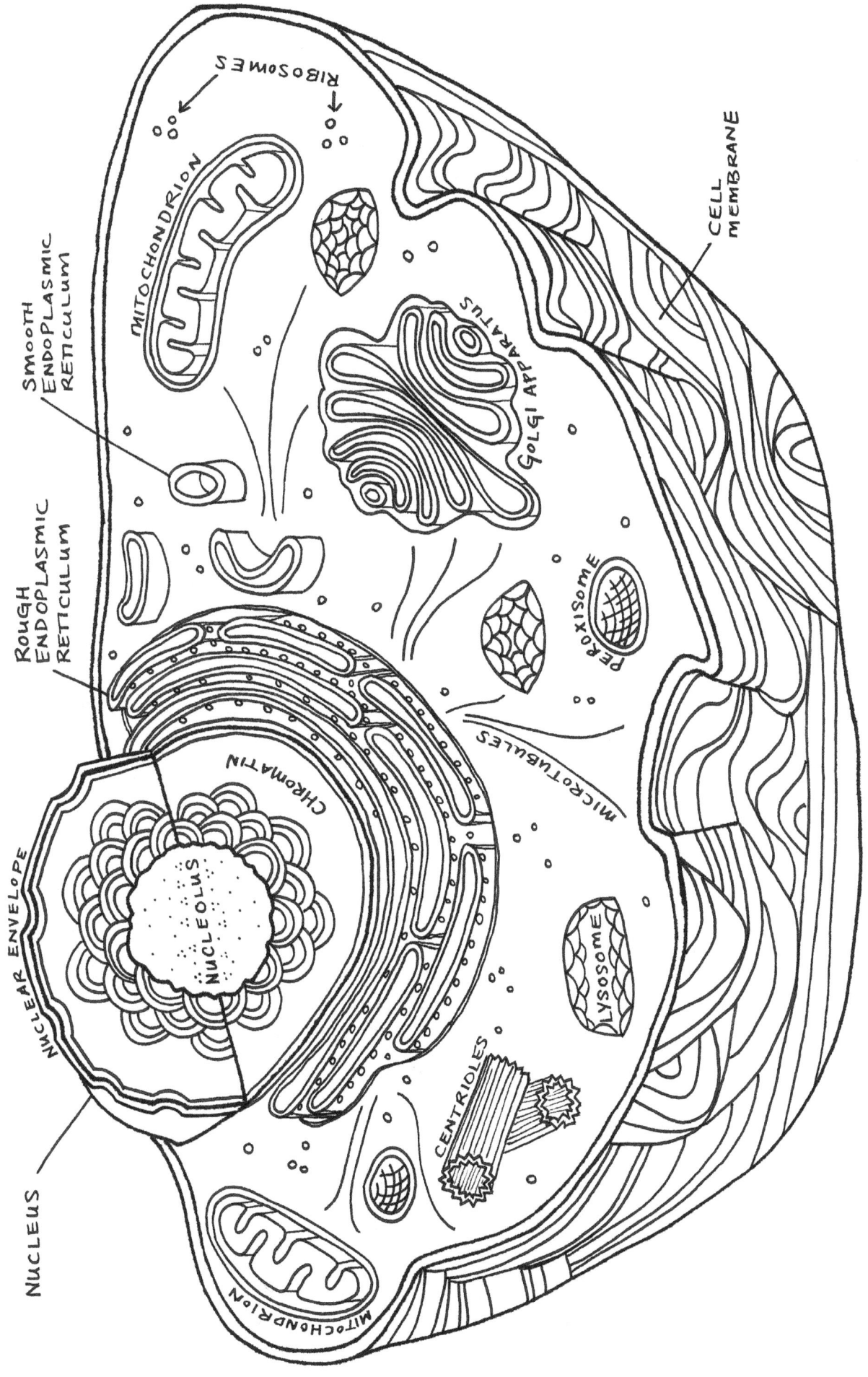

RIBOSOMES

MITOCHONDRION

SMOOTH ENDOPLASMIC RETICULUM

CELL MEMBRANE

GOLGI APPARATUS

PEROXISOME

MICROTUBULES

ROUGH ENDOPLASMIC RETICULUM

CHROMATIN

NUCLEAR ENVELOPE

NUCLEOLUS

NUCLEUS

LYSOSOME

CENTRIOLES

MITOCHONDRION

NOTES ★ SKETCHES ★ COLOR TESTS ★ COLOR CATCHER

NOTES ★ SKETCHES ★ COLOR TESTS ★ COLOR CATCHER

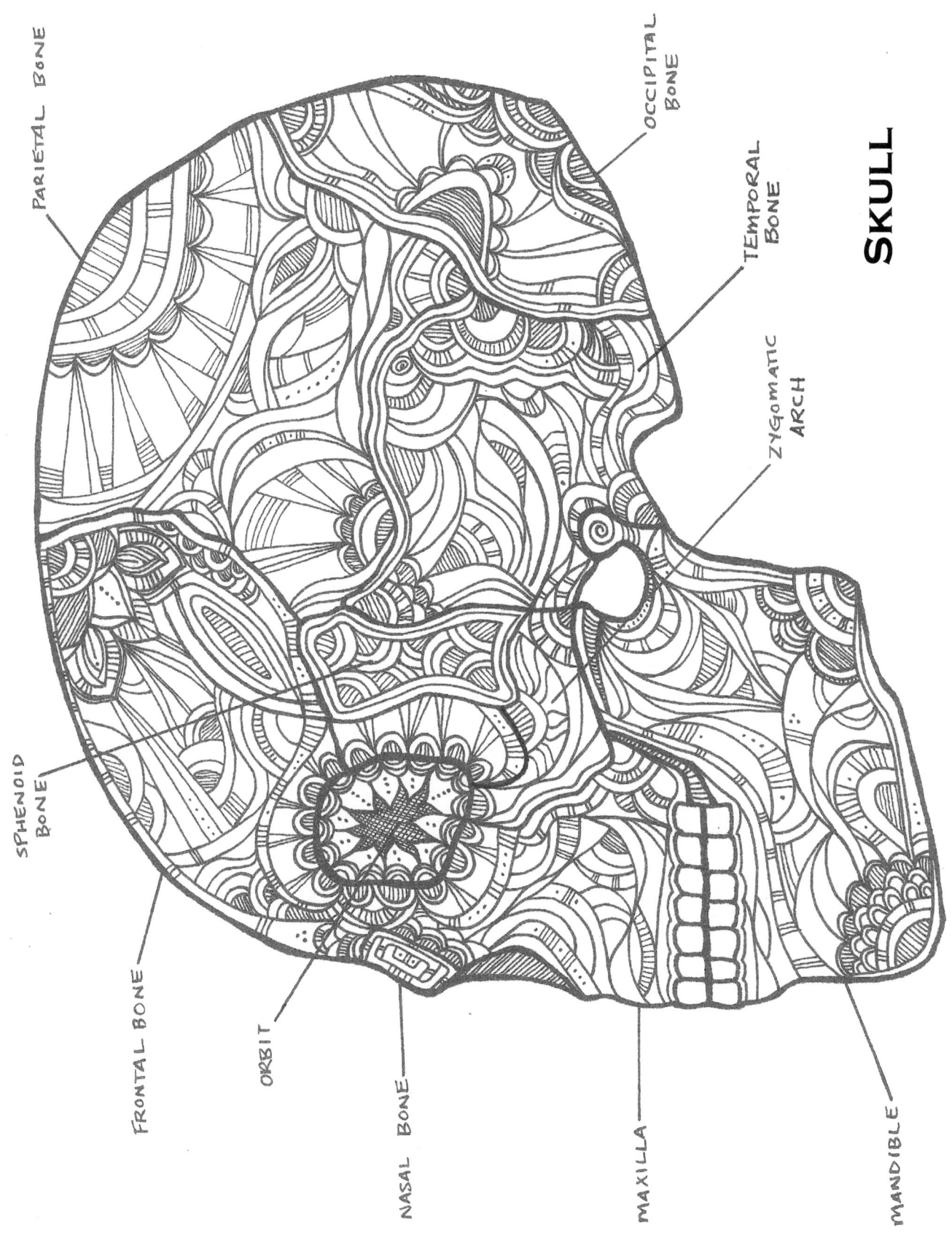

PARIETAL BONE

OCCIPITAL BONE

TEMPORAL BONE

ZYGOMATIC ARCH

SPHENOID BONE

FRONTAL BONE

ORBIT

NASAL BONE

MAXILLA

MANDIBLE

SKULL

NOTES ★ SKETCHES ★ COLOR TESTS ★ COLOR CATCHER

NOTES ★ SKETCHES ★ COLOR TESTS ★ COLOR CATCHER

BRAIN

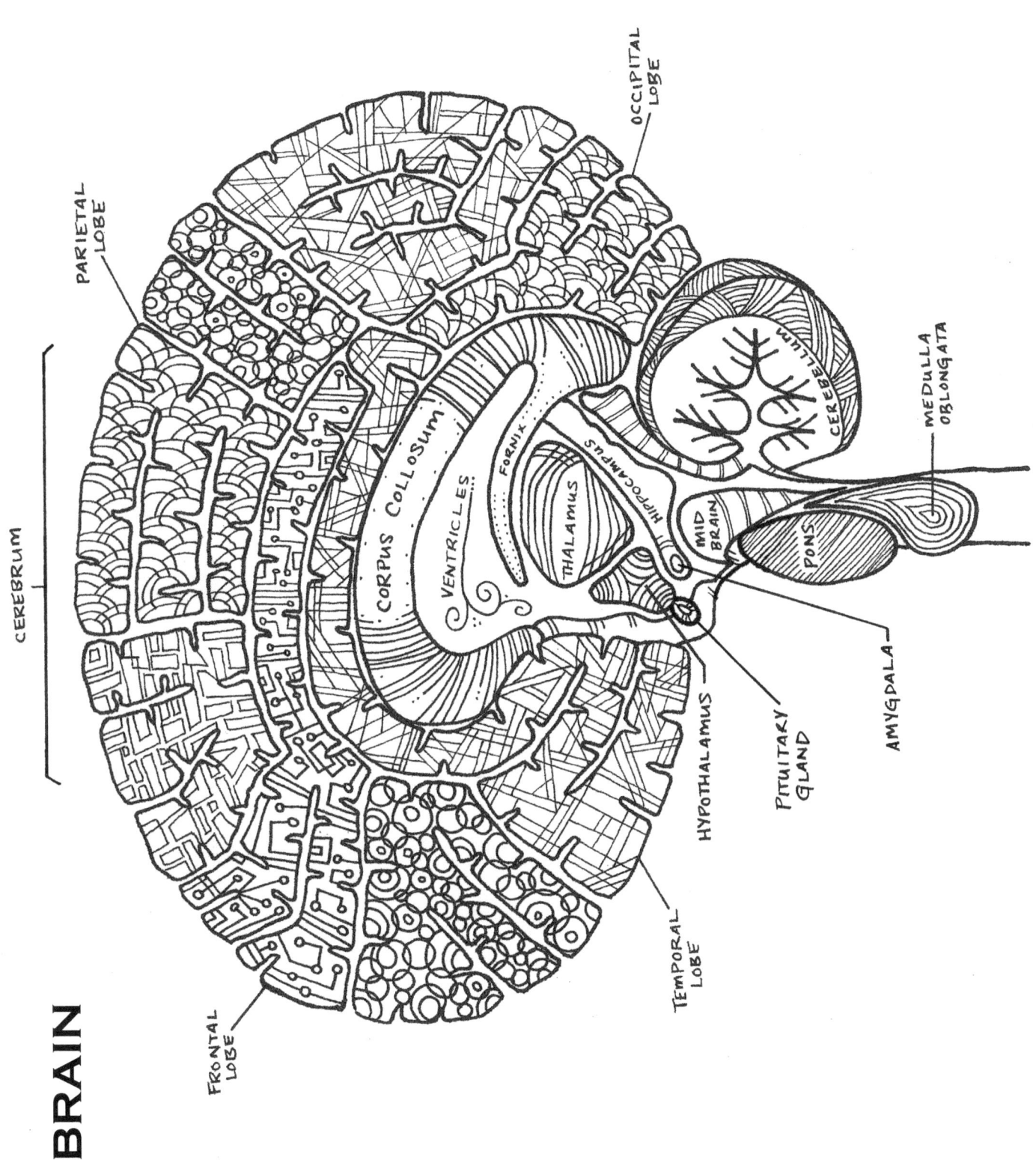

NOTES ★ SKETCHES ★ COLOR TESTS ★ COLOR CATCHER

NOTES ★ SKETCHES ★ COLOR TESTS ★ COLOR CATCHER

NEURON

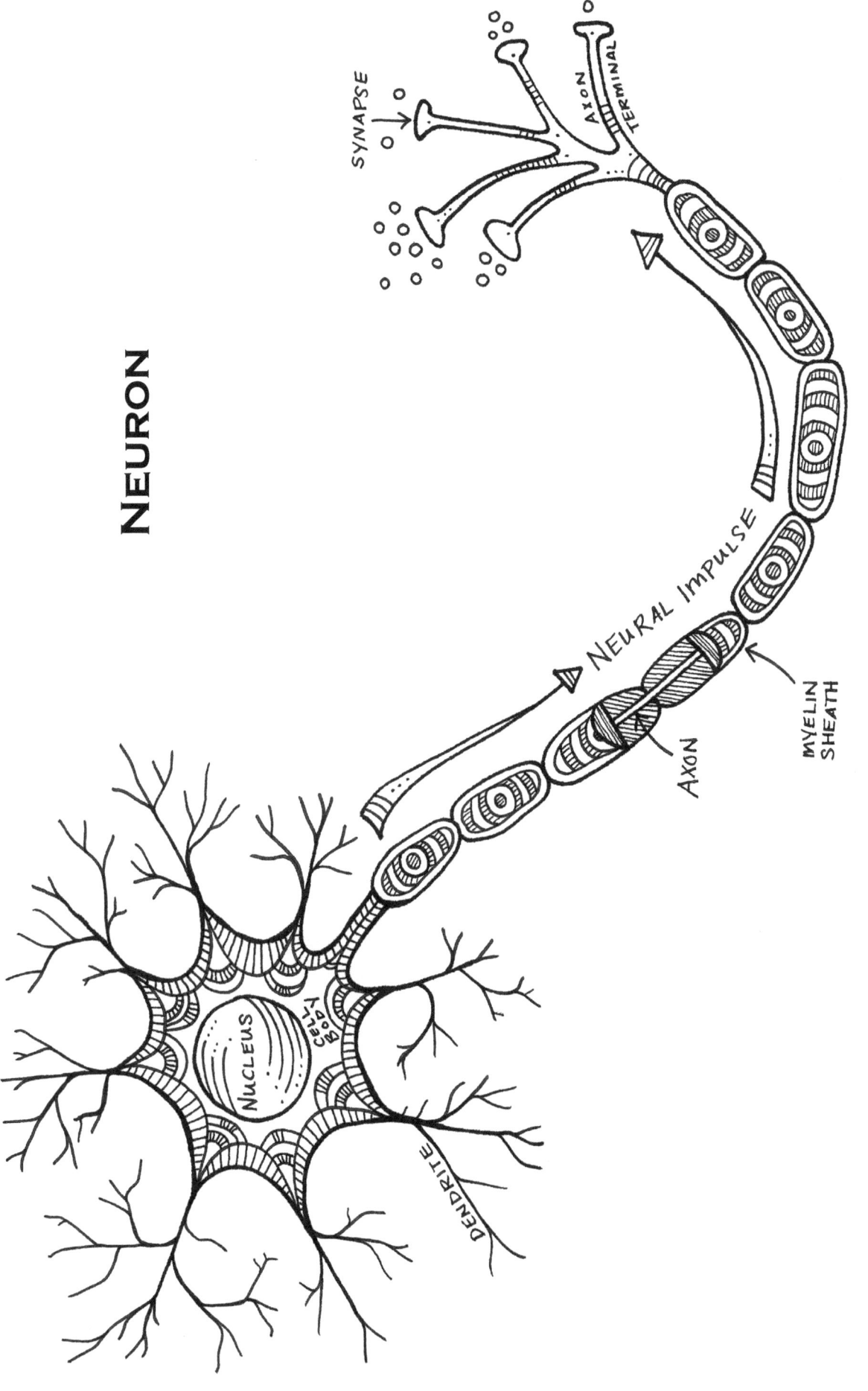

SYNAPSE

AXON TERMINAL

NEURAL IMPULSE

AXON

MYELIN SHEATH

NUCLEUS

CELL BODY

DENDRITE

NOTES ★ SKETCHES ★ COLOR TESTS ★ COLOR CATCHER

NOTES ★ SKETCHES ★ COLOR TESTS ★ COLOR CATCHER

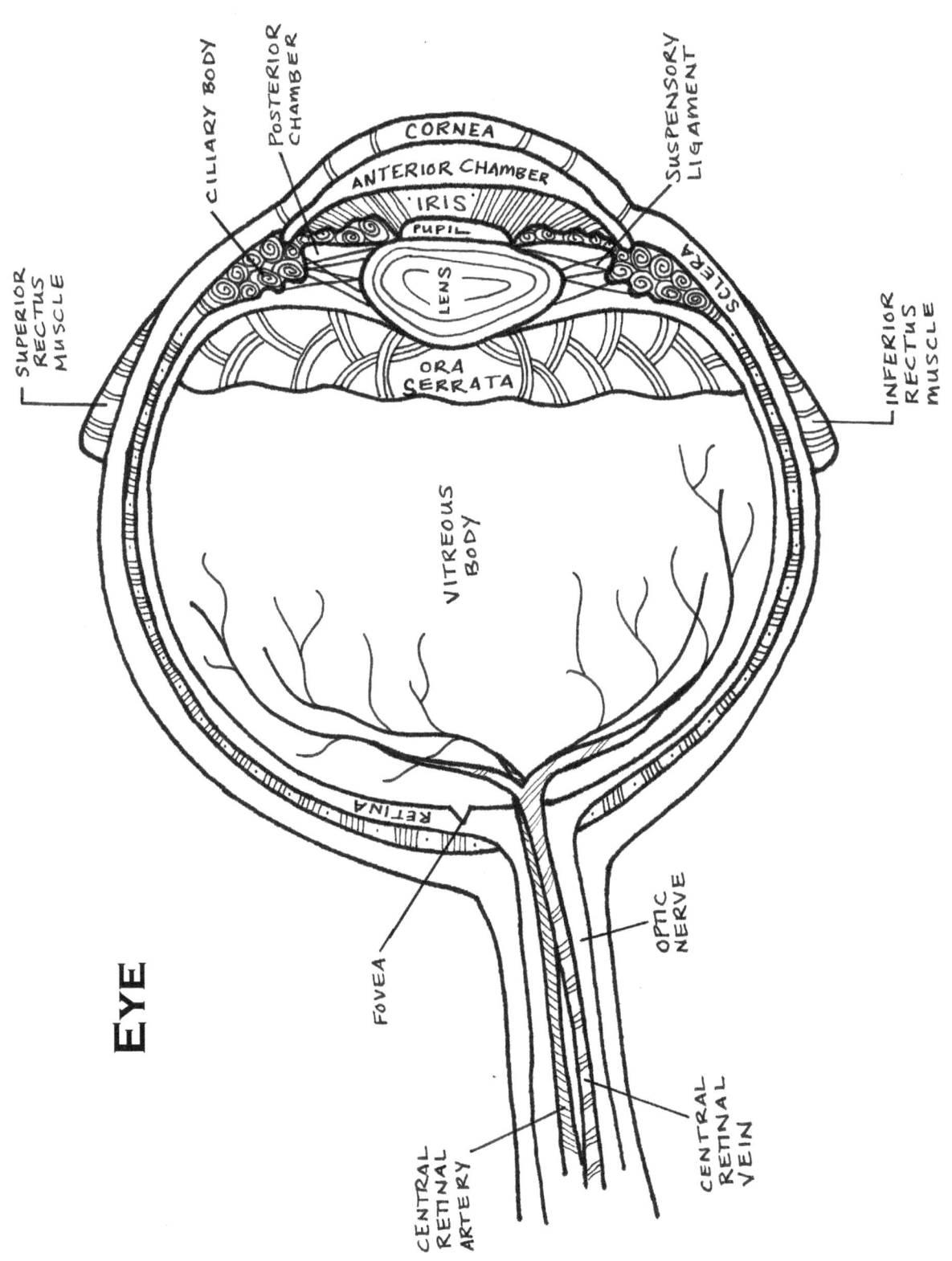

EYE

CORNEA

ANTERIOR CHAMBER

IRIS

PUPIL

LENS

ORA SERRATA

CILIARY BODY

POSTERIOR CHAMBER

SUSPENSORY LIGAMENT

SCLERA

SUPERIOR RECTUS MUSCLE

INFERIOR RECTUS MUSCLE

VITREOUS BODY

RETINA

FOVEA

OPTIC NERVE

CENTRAL RETINAL ARTERY

CENTRAL RETINAL VEIN

NOTES ★ SKETCHES ★ COLOR TESTS ★ COLOR CATCHER

NOTES ★ SKETCHES ★ COLOR TESTS ★ COLOR CATCHER

INNER EAR

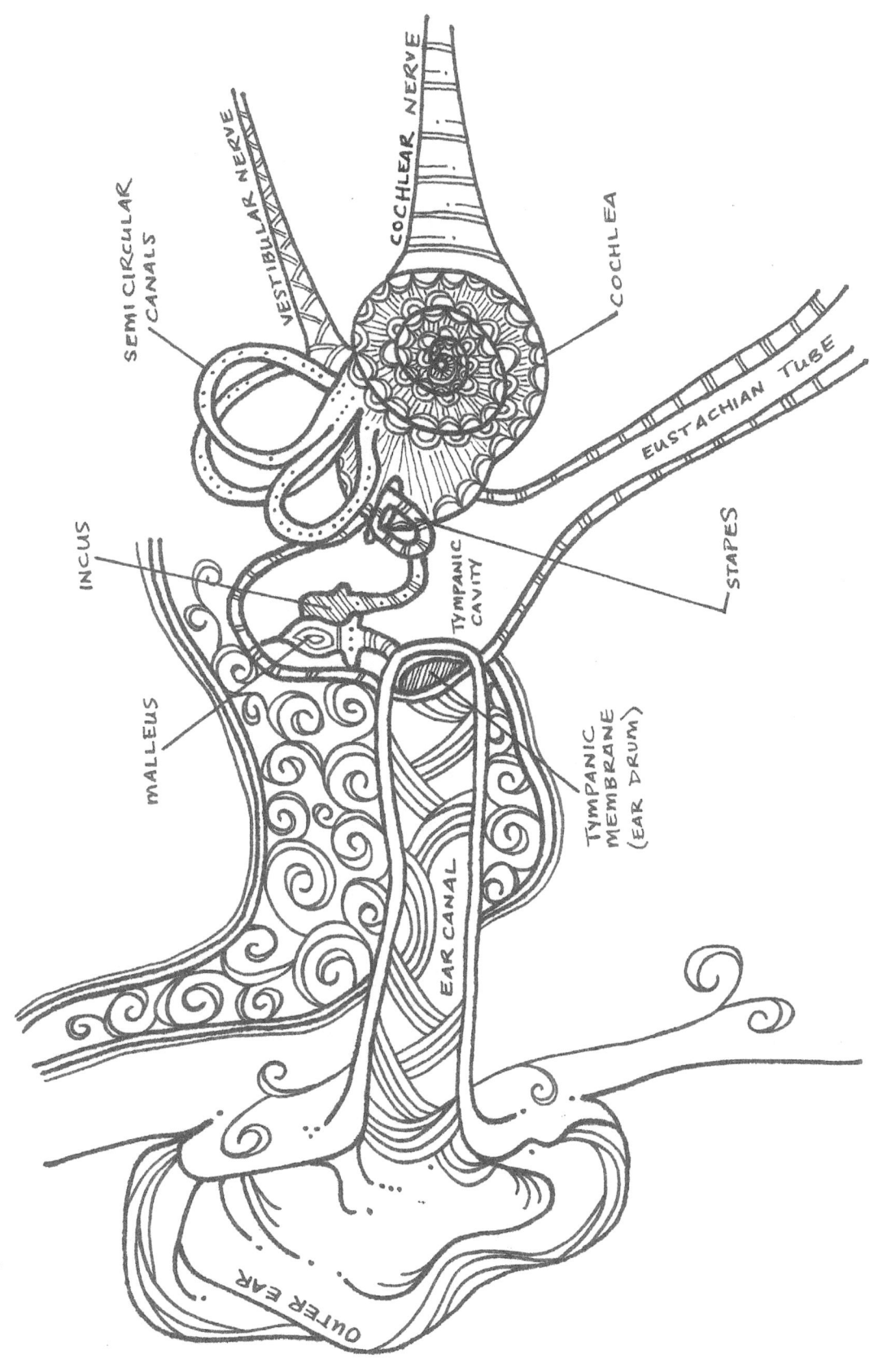

SEMICIRCULAR CANALS

VESTIBULAR NERVE

COCHLEAR NERVE

COCHLEA

EUSTACHIAN TUBE

STAPES

INCUS

TYMPANIC CAVITY

TYMPANIC MEMBRANE (EAR DRUM)

MALLEUS

EAR CANAL

OUTER EAR

NOTES ★ SKETCHES ★ COLOR TESTS ★ COLOR CATCHER

NOTES * SKETCHES * COLOR TESTS * COLOR CATCHER

Tooth

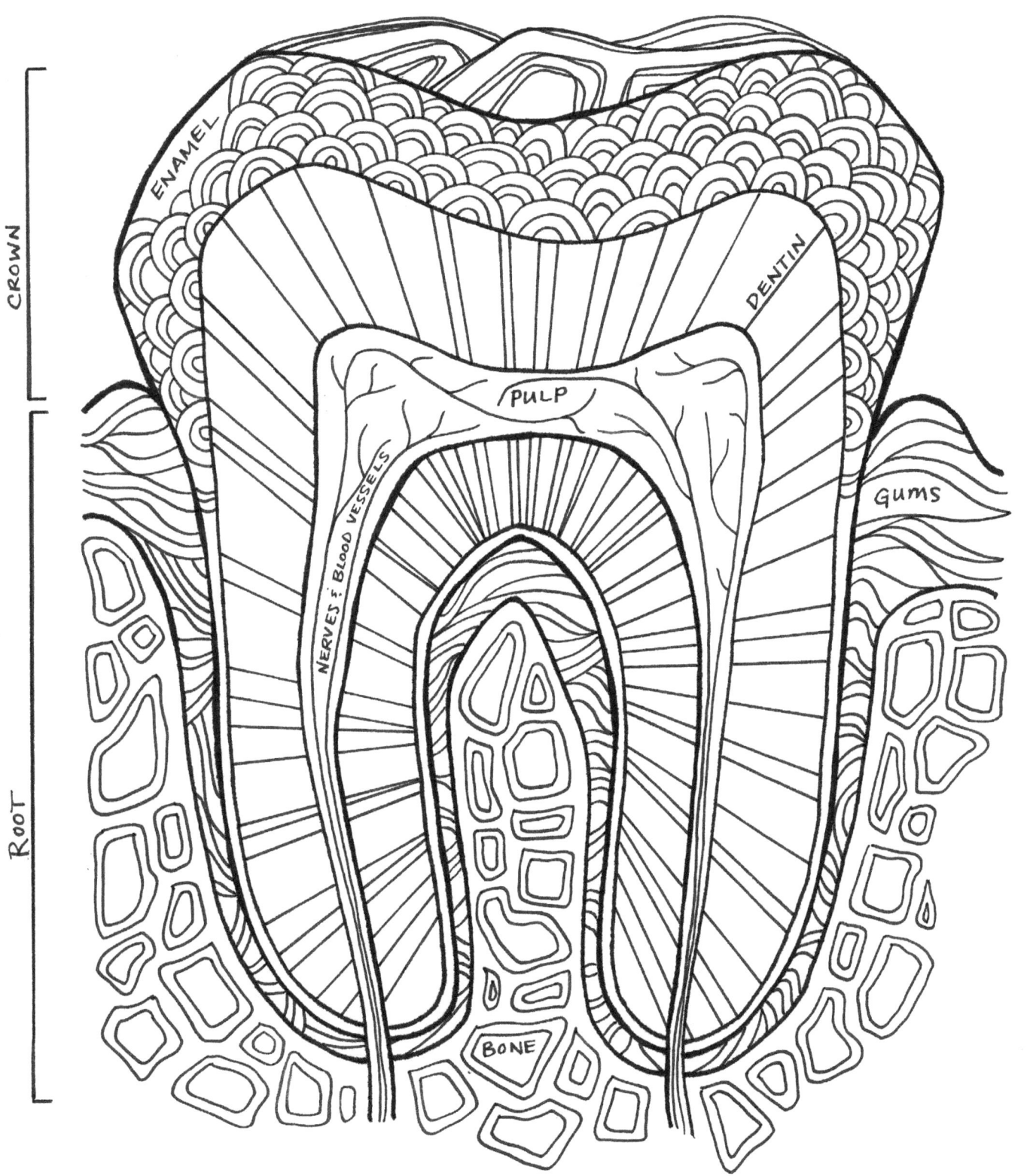

NOTES ★ SKETCHES ★ COLOR TESTS ★ COLOR CATCHER

NOTES ★ SKETCHES ★ COLOR TESTS ★ COLOR CATCHER

SKIN

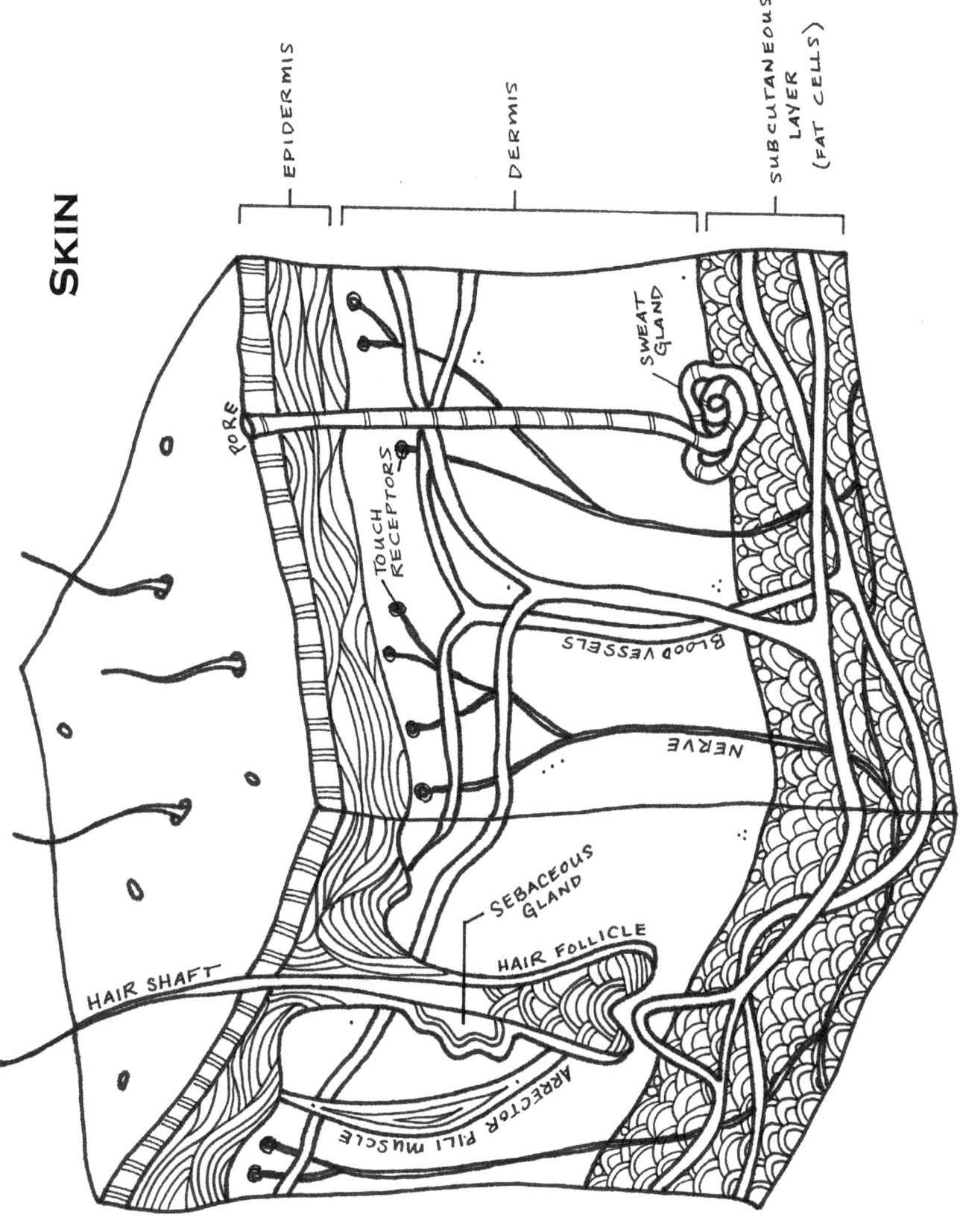

EPIDERMIS

DERMIS

SUBCUTANEOUS LAYER (FAT CELLS)

HAIR SHAFT

PORE

TOUCH RECEPTORS

SWEAT GLAND

BLOOD VESSELS

NERVE

SEBACEOUS GLAND

HAIR FOLLICLE

ARRECTOR PILI MUSCLE

NOTES ★ SKETCHES ★ COLOR TESTS ★ COLOR CATCHER

NOTES ★ SKETCHES ★ COLOR TESTS ★ COLOR CATCHER

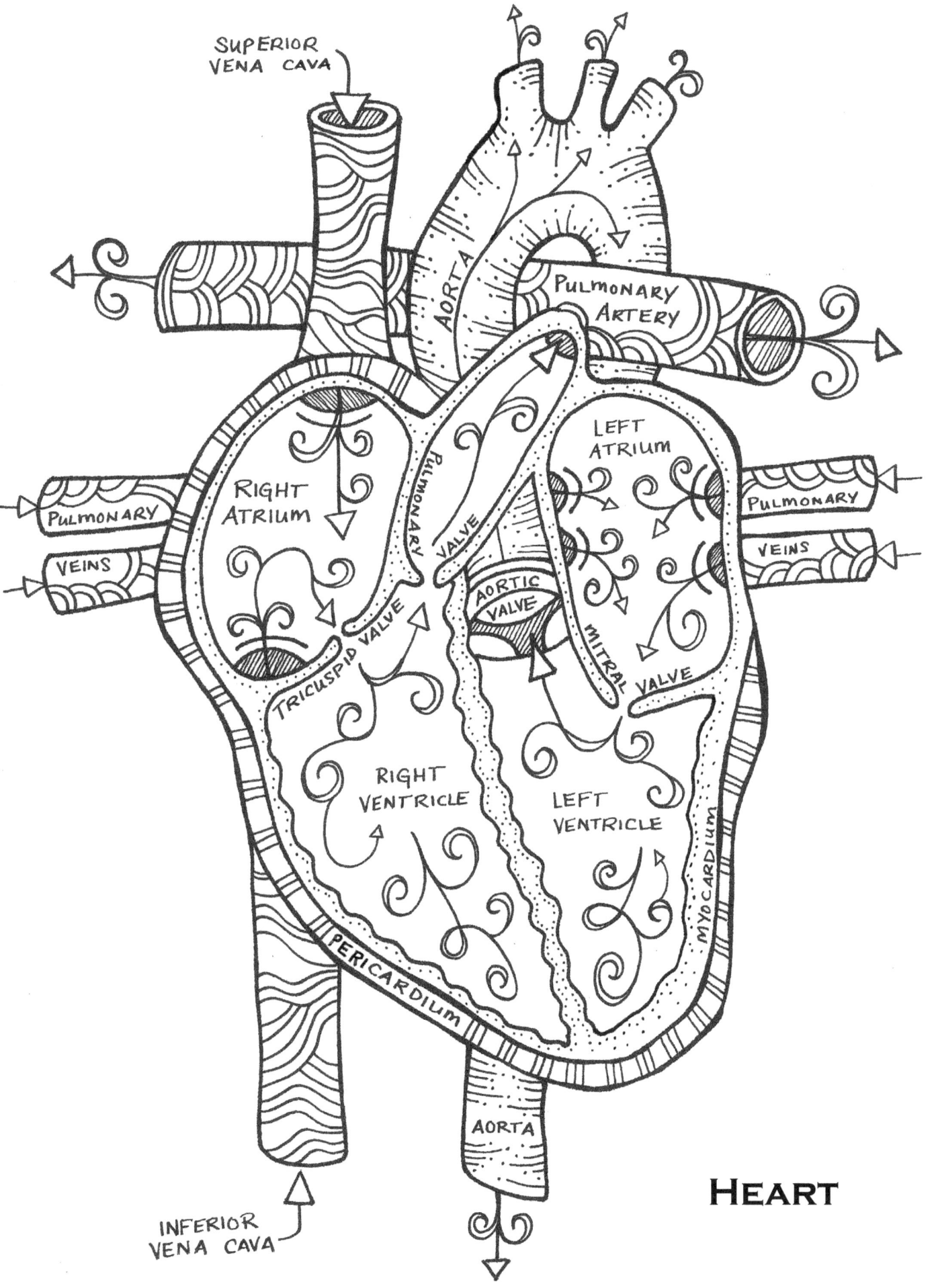

SUPERIOR
VENA CAVA

AORTA

PULMONARY
ARTERY

PULMONARY

VEINS

RIGHT
ATRIUM

PULMONARY
VALVE

LEFT
ATRIUM

PULMONARY

VEINS

AORTIC
VALVE

MITRAL
VALVE

TRICUSPID VALVE

RIGHT
VENTRICLE

LEFT
VENTRICLE

MYOCARDIUM

PERICARDIUM

AORTA

INFERIOR
VENA CAVA

HEART

NOTES ★ SKETCHES ★ COLOR TESTS ★ COLOR CATCHER

NOTES ★ SKETCHES ★ COLOR TESTS ★ COLOR CATCHER

LUNGS

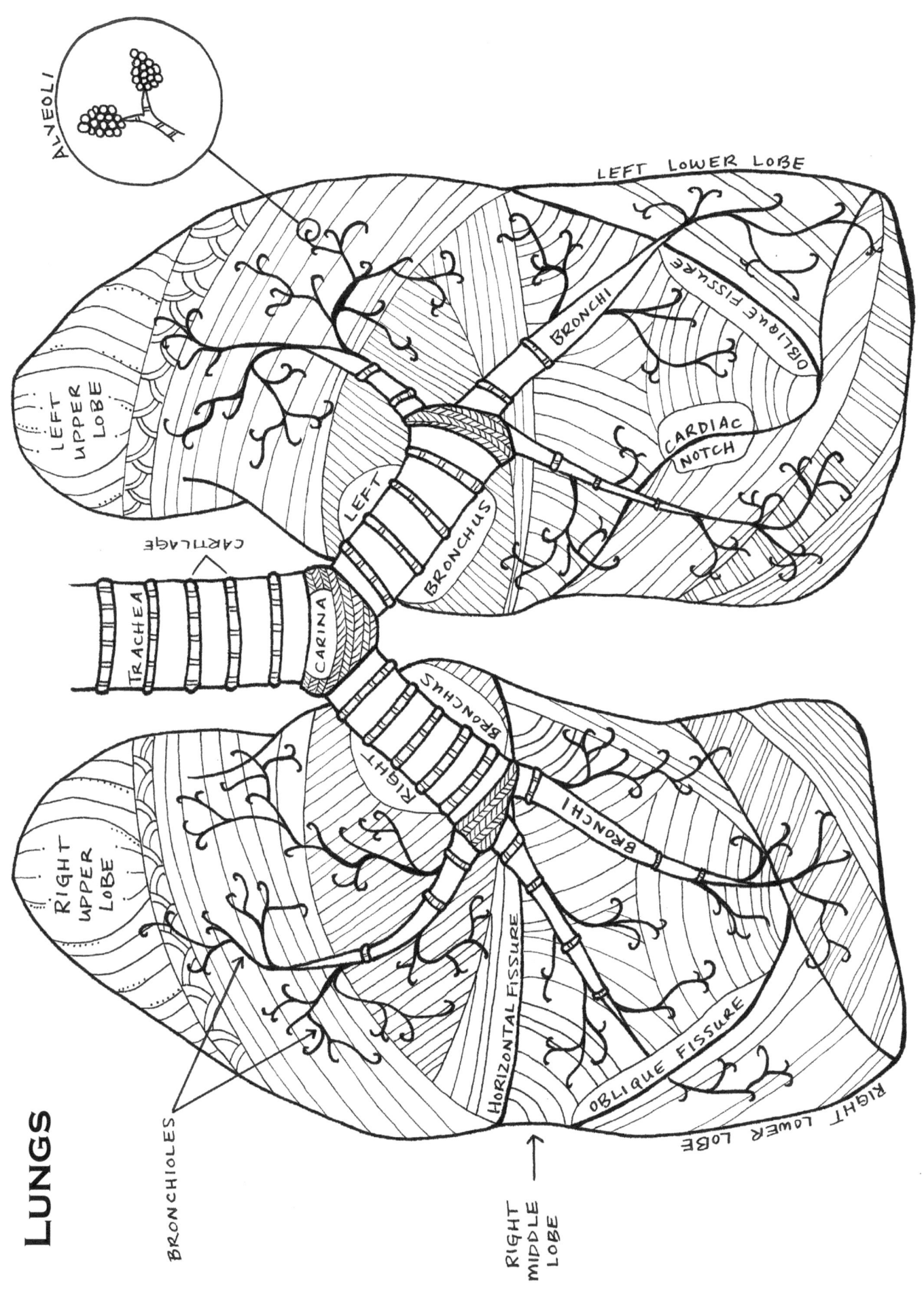

ALVEOLI

LEFT LOWER LOBE

BRONCHI

OBLIQUE FISSURE

CARDIAC NOTCH

LEFT UPPER LOBE

LEFT BRONCHUS

CARTILAGE

TRACHEA

CARINA

RIGHT BRONCHUS

RIGHT

BRONCHI

RIGHT UPPER LOBE

BRONCHIOLES

HORIZONTAL FISSURE

OBLIQUE FISSURE

RIGHT LOWER LOBE

RIGHT MIDDLE LOBE

NOTES * SKETCHES * COLOR TESTS * COLOR CATCHER

NOTES ★ SKETCHES ★ COLOR TESTS ★ COLOR CATCHER

KIDNEY

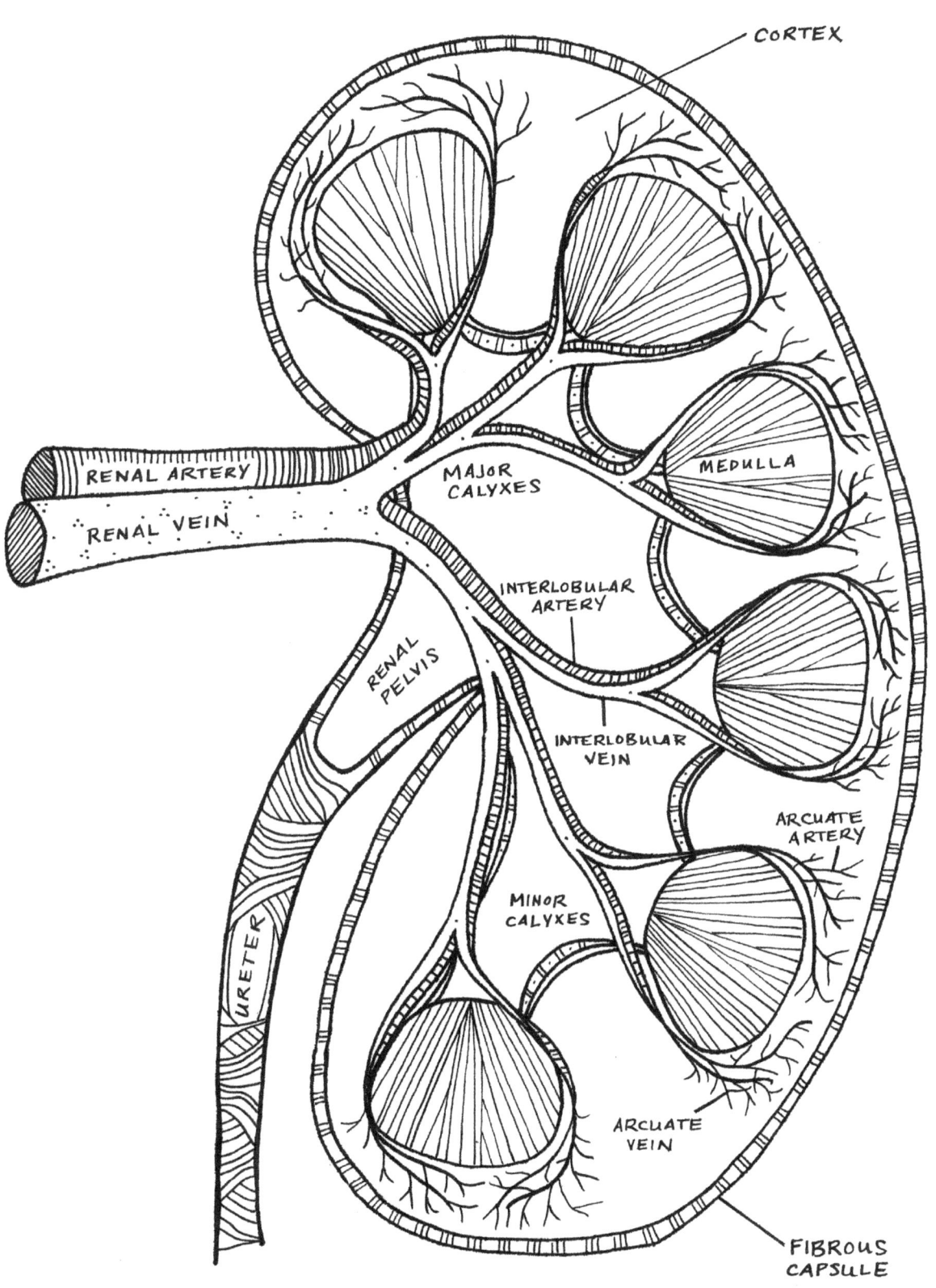

CORTEX

MEDULLA

MAJOR CALYXES

RENAL ARTERY

RENAL VEIN

INTERLOBULAR ARTERY

RENAL PELVIS

INTERLOBULAR VEIN

ARCUATE ARTERY

MINOR CALYXES

URETER

ARCUATE VEIN

FIBROUS CAPSULE

NOTES * SKETCHES * COLOR TESTS * COLOR CATCHER

NOTES ★ SKETCHES ★ COLOR TESTS ★ COLOR CATCHER

Digestive System

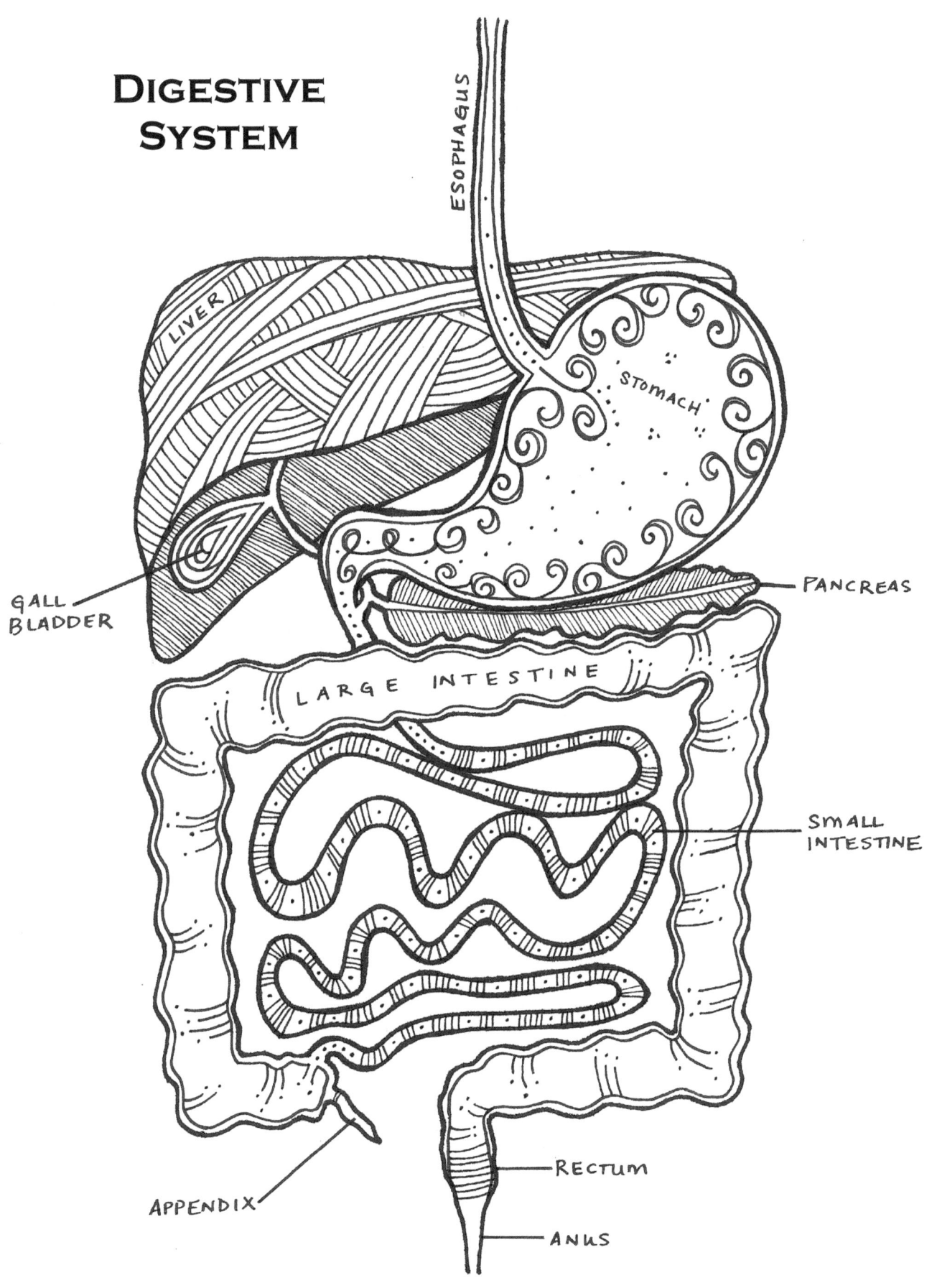

ESOPHAGUS

LIVER

STOMACH

GALL BLADDER

PANCREAS

LARGE INTESTINE

SMALL INTESTINE

APPENDIX

RECTUM

ANUS

NOTES ★ SKETCHES ★ COLOR TESTS ★ COLOR CATCHER

NOTES ★ SKETCHES ★ COLOR TESTS ★ COLOR CATCHER

BONES OF THE HAND

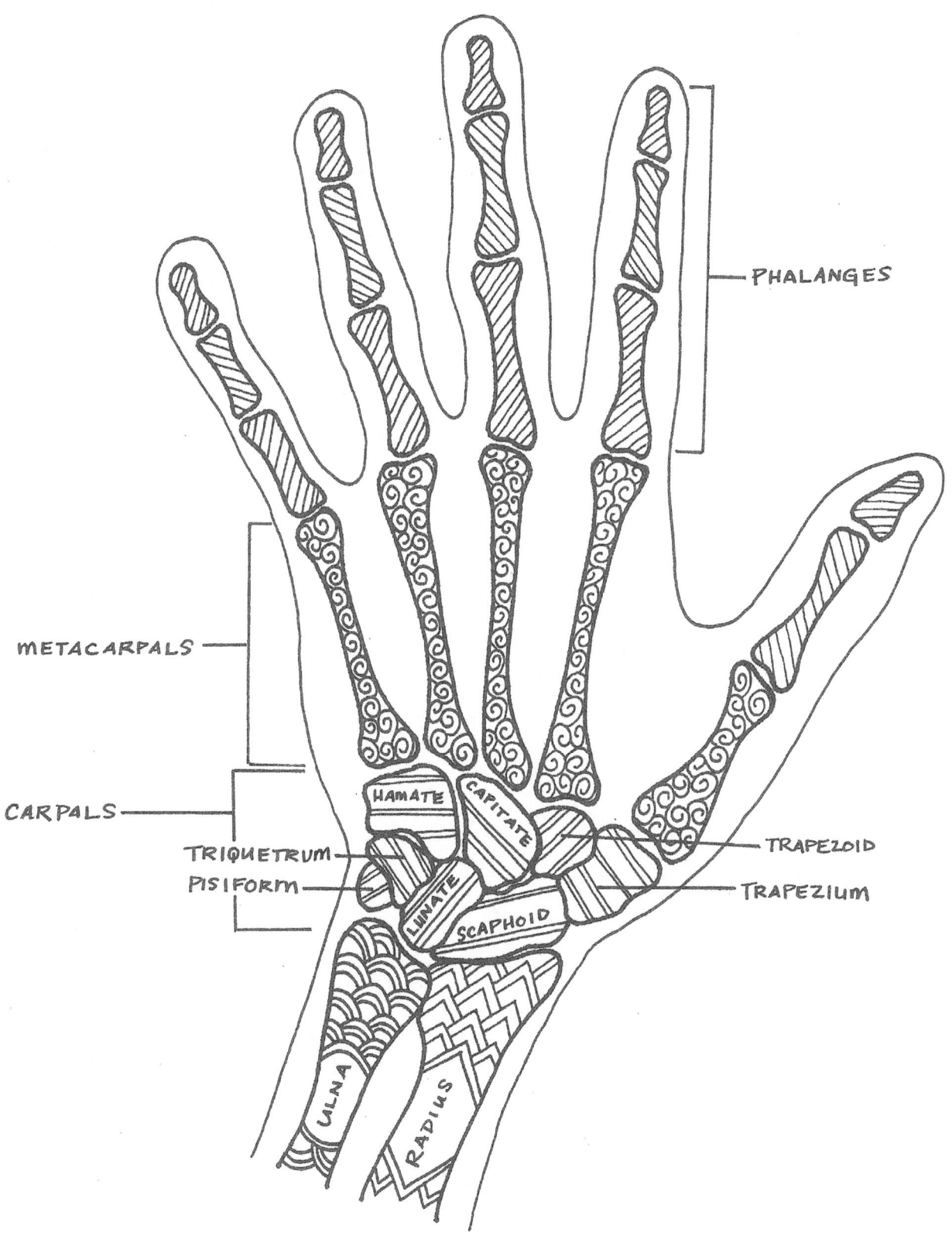

PHALANGES

METACARPALS

CARPALS

TRIQUETRUM

PISIFORM

HAMATE

CAPITATE

TRAPEZOID

TRAPEZIUM

LUNATE

SCAPHOID

ULNA

RADIUS

NOTES ★ SKETCHES ★ COLOR TESTS ★ COLOR CATCHER

NOTES ★ SKETCHES ★ COLOR TESTS ★ COLOR CATCHER

BONES OF THE FOOT

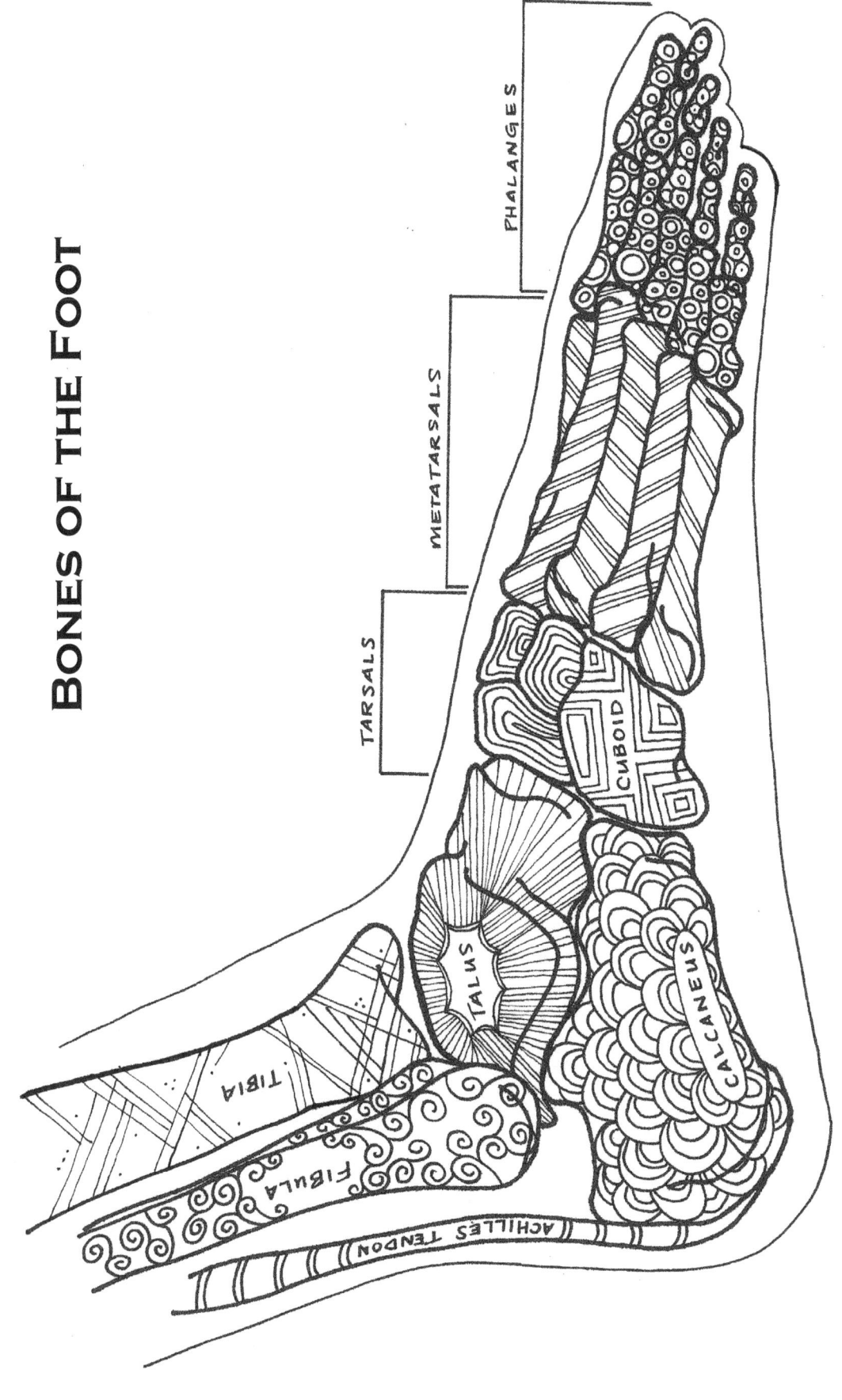

PHALANGES

METATARSALS

TARSALS

CUBOID

TALUS

CALCANEUS

TIBIA

FIBULA

(ACHILLES TENDON)

NOTES * SKETCHES * COLOR TESTS * COLOR CATCHER

NOTES ★ SKETCHES ★ COLOR TESTS ★ COLOR CATCHER

I hope you enjoyed your journey through
ART of the HEART and other Anatomical Structures!

For more art from AMY GRACE SLOAN please visit
www.amygraceri.wix.com/decorateyourlife

or

www.facebook.com/AmyGraceSloan